God's Love
EASTER POEMS

GOD'S LOVE – EASTER POEMS
Text Copyright 2018 by Richard I. Gold

All rights reserved. No part of this book may be reproduced or transmitted in any form or by any means, electronic or mechanical, including photocopying, recording, or by any information storage and retrieval system without written permission from the publisher or the author. The only exception is brief quotations for reviews.

For information address:

J2B Publishing LLC
4251 Columbia Park Road
Pomfret, MD 20675
www.J2BLLC.com
GladToDoIt@gmail.com

Printed and bound in the United States of America.
This book is set in Bookman Old Style. Designed by Mary Barrows.

Background cover image used under license from Shutterstock.com
Background texture by: ilolab
ID: 117941473

ISBN: 978-1-948747-00-4 - Paperback
       978-1-948747-01-1 - Hardcover
       978-1-948747-07-3 - Ebook

God's Love
Easter Poems

Richard I. Gold

Also by Richard I. Gold

God's Agenda - Religious Poems - Vol 1

Mary's Lamb and other Christmas Poems

Sayings for the Believer

EOD and War Poems

- Dedication -

These poems are dedicated to my wife, Penelope (Penny) Gold, who has supported me in my efforts to product and publish these poems.

The author wishes to thank his cousin James Greenlee, Jim Brewster and Ms. Debby Holder who have reviewed the poems for spelling and wording. However, if there are any errors the author takes full responsibility.

TABLE OF CONTENTS

INTRODUCTION	1
HOW GREAT IS THE LOVE OF GOD	2
GOD'S LOVE	4
EASTER	6
LONG AGO	8
WE CANNOT KNOW THE END OF LIFE	10
THE ONE AND ONLY GOD	11
WHEN EVIL MEN	12
BORN TO DIE	14
THE COMING OF THE CHRIST	16
FOR REASONS WE CAN NEVER KNOW	18
THE SON OF GOD GOES FORTH TO WAR	20
IF GOD BE FOR US	21
THERE IS BUT ONE WAY	22
GOD'S CARE	24
INTO THE VALLEY OF DEATH	25
OUR NEW RELATION WITH GOD	26
INTO THE WORLD	27
DO WE KNOW WHY MEN MUST DIE?	28
THE WILL OF GOD	29
MEN ON EARTH	30
WORLD IN TURMOIL	32
THE WORLD OF MAN	33

GOD CHOOSE TO WORK WITH MEN	34
HOW DO WE GET TO HEAVEN?	35
THE BEGINNING OF ALL THINGS NEW	36
GOD SENT HIS SON	38
DO YOU REMEMBER?	40
WE MUST DO THE WORK	42
WHY SHOULD THE HOLY GOD	44
LIMITED MEN AND WOMEN	46
THE MERCY OF GOD	48
IN THE WAR WITH EVIL	50
WHERE IS THE LOVE OF GOD	52
IN THE WAR FOR THE SOULS OF MEN	53
STRUGGLE FOR RIGHT	54
WHAT CAN WE GIVE GOD?	56
MEN ARE A SELFISH LOT	58
ONE WAY AND ONLY ONE	59
WHEN GOD, THE ETERNAL KING	60
DO YOU KNOW MY GOD?	62
CRY, CRY, CRY	63
CHRISTIANS COMMEMORATE EASTER DAY	64
THE LANGUAGE OF HEAVEN	65
IN A TIME LONG AGO	66
LET US PRAISE THE LORD	68
THE WILL OF GOD	70
LET NOT YOUR DESIRE	72
HOW DO WE COUNT OUR WEALTH	74
WE WISH TO KNOW	76

THE HOPE WE ALL HAVE	77
MISSION TO MANKIND	78
WHAT DO YOU BELIEVE	80
TO WHAT DO WE OWE OUR ALLEGIANCE?	82
WHAT IS EASTER TO YOU?	83
WHENEVER EVIL STRIKES	84
WHENEVER WE THINK OF GOD	86
NO MATTER HOW BAD	88
THE WAY TO HEAVEN	90
THE WORLD OF MEN WAS WAITING	91
BEFORE THE AGE OF MAN	92
IN THE BEGINNING	94
MEN SENT BY GOD	95
CAN PEOPLE FIND THE TRUTH	96
BLESS OUR HOLY GOD	98
IF GOD WERE A MAN	99
HEAVEN'S REVOLUTION	100
THERE ARE MANY WAYS	102
REJOICE	104
THE FORCES OF EVIL	106
THE SUN COMES UP	107
PRAISE THE LORD	108
THE TIME HAS COME	110
INTO THIS WORLD	112
THE WORKING OF GOD	114
ALL PEOPLE HAVE SINNED	115
GOD'S TIME	116

PRAISE THE LORD	118
THE SPRING OF THE YEAR	120
THERE ARE THINGS I WOULD DO	122
ACCEPTED BY GOD'S SON	123
WHAT IS A CHRISTIAN?	124
IN ALL THE WORLD	126
SOME PEOPLE WANT GOD	128
NO MAN CAN EVER BE GOD	129
A LAND FAR AWAY	130
MADE RIGHT WITH GOD	132
HOW CAN THE HUMAN MIND	134
GOD'S MERCY	136
PRAISE BE TO GOD	138
THE MIND OF GOD	140
EASTER IS A COMBINATION	141
THE BRIGHT MORNING	142
WHEN WE THINK OF OUR HOLY GOD	144
SERVE THE LORD WITH GLADNESS	146
THE FUTURE IS BRIGHT	148
LIFE'S PATH	149
HELP	150
THE BEGINNING OF THE WILL OF GOD	152
THE WILL OF GOD	154
THERE IS BUT ONE WAY TO HEAVEN	156
ALL PEOPLE MUST WORK	158
FOLLOW HIS TEACHINGS	159

x

- INTRODUCTION -

Easter is both a celebration and a commemoration of the life and death of one Man, Jesus Christ. These poems commemorate His life, teachings, death, and resurrection and His influence on our life, our society, the world, and history.

In places, the term" man" or "men" has been used to refer to all humans; in the past, the present and the future. We are all responsible, both men and women, to God above and to our fellow humans.

Before Christians were labeled "Christians," they were referred to as "The People of the Way." The instances in these poems where the word "Way" capitalized, the use indicates Christians.

HOW GREAT IS THE LOVE OF GOD

How great is the love of God
For the children of men
That we should receive salvation
When His Son He did send

What could we have done
To deserve so great a gift
From God, the Almighty Lord
To be lifted from eternity's rift

There is no reason we can know
That God should care for us
But as we wander through our life
It must be in God we trust

Let us rejoice in this great love
From Him we thankfully receive
Given by the One on high
For His mercy we truly need

There is but one way of salvation
Given to the children of men
To live it communion with God
So that at death to heaven God will send

We must trust today in mercy
That the Holy One does send
Cause the sacrifice of the Holy One
Allows our soul's evil to mend

GOD'S LOVE

To this world of toil and sin
God sent His holy Son
To give us hope and salvation
To show His love had begun

Men valued not this holy prize
They should love and hold in awe
They rejected the love of God
They ignored the love they saw

Today many men think the same
Ignoring what men of old knew
That by the power of God's own hand
The Son did show what's true

Look at this world and weep for men
Who accept not God's holy love
We pray that their inmost self
May be accepted by heaven above

Men and women are not holy
Can never be while on earth
Unless their souls be made anew
By the spirit's holy birth

What we say of the love of God?
Holy and just from above
Who for reasons not known to men
Displays to all His eternal love

The love of God is holy
The love of God is pure
The love of God for us
We know it is sure

Pray to our Holy God
Pray to be made whole
That when our life does end
God takes to Heaven our soul

EASTER

Easter is a unique celebration
When we remember the Holy Man
Who came from God above
To teach us God's loving hand

There is nothing like this
In any of the world's other faiths
The basis of the Christian's life
Is God's eternal grace

The Holy Man sent by God
To tell His message to men
That by the grace of God
Our salvation can begin

This Man was killed in a cruel way
Hung upon a bloody tree
By evil, godless men
We may ask "What does this mean to me?"

When He died upon that cross
He was placed in the grave
For those who followed Him
Wandered about the assurance He gave

But God did not leave Jesus dead
God raised Him to life anew
That all who believe might be saved
With the eternal grace so true

For His disciples a joyous time
An event like none other
For God showed His grace
And His eternal power

Our hope in God's grace
It is forever with us
For in this Way we hope
We eternally trust

LONG AGO

Long ago in a land far away
The holy God came down
In the body of a Man
Salvation's trumpet to sound

The Man taught us the Way
To be pleasing to our God
We are to tell all men
Before we end beneath the sod

As it was then
So it is now
He showed us life
He taught us how

There is but one Way
Known to the children of men
To be made right with God
He showed us how to begin

But from the beginning
Until the very end
God wants us to follow His Way
And refrain from every sin

So let us follow His Way
The Way that is of God
We must follow in His steps
As on life's path we trod

When we find the way of God
Do as He would have us do
We can rest eternally assured
That our eternal life is true

WE CANNOT KNOW THE END OF LIFE

We cannot know the end of life
Or how we will meet our Maker
But we can know the way to walk
Before we need an undertaker

If we truly know what we must do
In every passing day
We would never sin
Or need the Son's life to pay

But we are not perfect
We can but praise the God of love
That He cared so for us
He sent His Son from above

When He came to teach us the Way
To live as God would have us live
It is the blessings of God
That to this child He did give

THE ONE AND ONLY GOD

The one and only God
Sent His only Son
To guide and keep us
So on life's path we may run

There were many days of life
That He lived upon this earth
Told us how to please God
By living the Second Birth

It was many years ago
The Son of God did live
The teachings God given through Him
His life for us He did give

So worship the Father
Through Jesus Christ the Son
We may be made right with God
When, for us, eternity has begun

WHEN EVIL MEN

When evil men
Killed the Son of God
They thought they had won
Satan gave them the nod

Men cannot understand God's purpose
Something they could never know
They found from the eternal God
There is an eternal way to go

When the Son was placed in the tomb
They found that God works were true
God raised Him from the grave
By His power He gave Jesus life anew

We can go against the will of God
We can do the evil that we will
We think that it is a joy
But the end is eternally ill

No matter whom we are
If no one can stand against us
We may think that we have it all
That all else is a bust

But we can never know
The will of God for us
It is in the power of the Holy God
That all good men must trust

For victory of the evil one
Is what those evil ones trust
They come to an evil end
For those who are against God and us

So worship our Holy God
Worship in every way
Follow His teachings
Every hour of every day

BORN TO DIE

When Jesus was born in Bethlehem
By love He was cradled in hay
Men did not know why He came
Did not know He'd teach God's Way

Born in weakness was God's plan
To set the life of the gentle child
God sent Him to teach us how to live
Our relations to men should be mild

When He had grown to be a man
He taught the children of men
The way to be made right with God
By the holy will a new life to begin

When He had completed His work
Evil men took Him to the cross
They thought that through His death
That it would be God's loss

Then God showed His power
Raised Christ from the dead
That we may be made holy
And Hell's fury not dread

For He showed us the Second Birth
That by God's holy will
We may live as we ought
Evil against us not to prevail

No man may know the Holy Way
But only by God's Holy Son
That when our life does end
Heaven's race we will have run

While we are on earth
From the beginning till the end
We should be God's holy ones
So that salvation may begin

THE COMING OF THE CHRIST

The coming of the Christ
Was not a holy hit and run
But the new age of God
For mankind had begun

God is the power for all men
That controls all we do
So let us know His holy will
Make sure that we are true

There is no other way
To find God's holy will
In this life or the next
Our hope, our goodness to fulfill

No man has seen God's holy face
No man could see and live
So let us worship His Holy Self
Bless Him for all the good he will give

God and men control this earth
Control means we must care
For how we live our life
Should not damage more than earth can bare

Know we are responsible
For our earth and fellow men
We shall be judged in eternity
For the results we rend

FOR REASONS WE CAN NEVER KNOW

For reasons we can never know
God chose to care for the children of men
Has chosen to show us the way to live
Gave His Son so we can know how to begin

God's Son came into the world
Born a helpless babe
When He became a man
He showed the Way God gave

He worked with the children of men
To show us God's way to save
Taught Men the will of God
The Holy Way He gave

In order to live in the Way of God
He taught and lived and healed
As He went about doing good
It seemed God's will was sealed

Then in the unjust world
He was killed by evil men
Bound Upon a wicked cross
For the forgiveness of our sin

In the cold dark grave
Christ lay for two days
His people had lost hope
They could not give God praise

In order to show His power
God raised Christ to life anew
To give authority to all He taught
So we might live by the way that's true

Many years have passed
We can but follow in the Way
By the Son's life and death
For our sins Christ did pay

So walk the path of God
Walk it to the end
There is no other way
To be saved from sin

THE SON OF GOD GOES FORTH TO WAR

The Son of God goes forth to war
Against the unnumbered foe
The power of the hand of God
He carries as he doth go

But though the struggle is long and hard
Though we have many a trial
Victory is assured by the hand of God
Though our struggles are not mild

We must be loyal to our Holy King
His will we must seek
He will not settle for defeat
When we gather at His holy feet

IF GOD BE FOR US

If God be for us,
For our way of life
We must follow His will
To act as He would have us act
The Way of God to fulfill

We ask "Is God is on our side?"
But we should ask "Are we on God's side?"
For if God be for us, for our way of life
We can be sure with us He will abide

There are many the ways of men
Many for both bad and good
But let us so stand the test
That we do what we should

THERE IS BUT ONE WAY

There is one way and only one
To travel the path to God
It is by the life and death
Of Jesus Christ, our guiding Rod

We live but a short time on earth
Much there is to do
But by God's Holy Son
We will forever live
This is sure and true

We cannot go to heaven by doing good
We must follow in His Way
This is what we must do
But cross the line to the bad
Leaves us out of what is true

No man has crossed the great divide
From life to death and returned to life
Only the Holy Son
It was He the Holy God did send

So we must live by faith and hope
As eternity we seek
We walk this path of life
We must God's will keep

GOD'S CARE

God cared for all mankind
In His unending love
The greatest gift He could give
Was from heaven above

God sent His only Son
To pay for human sin
For those who will humbly submit
In God's will to begin

There could be no greater love
Of the almighty God
But to give us a way for eternal life
Before we're beneath the sod

God's Holy Will we must follow
To find His Holy Love
That by our life and by our works
Show all we follow God above

INTO THE VALLEY OF DEATH

Into the valley of death
Walked my Holy Lord
This path only He could trod
He was, He is the Holy Word

Our sins can be forgiven
Our sins against our Holy God
There was, there is, there can be no other
Who will carry our eternal load

So love God the Father
So love God the Son
By the power of the Holy Spirit
The race of life may be won

OUR NEW RELATION WITH GOD

Our new relation with God
Began with the death of His Son
The day Christ suffered for us
The glory that caused our soul to run

God gave of His Holy Self
When ere Jesus did begin
Came to teach and love and die
For the forgiveness of our sin

We can do nothing
To deserve what God has done
That we may to heaven go
When life's trails are won

INTO THE WORLD

Into this world stained by sin
God chose to send His only Son
Sent as a small helpless child
But by His life victory won

It is not the path I would choose
In the world of men
But God gave us a way
To be cleansed of our sin

It was the Way when the Son lived
It is the Way today
For without forgiveness of sin
It will be our soul we have to pay

So worship God in Heaven
Through Jesus Christ, His Son
Follow His instructions for life
As along life's path we run

DO WE KNOW WHY MEN MUST DIE?

Do we know why men must die?
Do we know why we must try?
Do we know why God loves mankind?
Do we know why we can never know why?

The workings of our Holy God
Sent His only Son to earth
To teach all men how to live
To give us the holy birth

It took the death
Of God's Holy Son
To make us acceptable to God
Ere eternity has begun

Men judge the actions of men
Men judge the actions of God
The first we must, the second a fool
For God sets the eternal rule

THE WILL OF GOD

The will of the Holy God
When we find it, how should we act?
God is our Father and our King
That is that, a fact

Often we want to find the easy way
The one that does not demand from us
That we would do what we will
But the end of this is an eternal bust

God knows what He is doing
Calling on us to follow His will
It is the only way
We can his agenda fulfill

MEN ON EARTH

The body we have on earth
Is a blessing from God
It is one all people have
To be used till we're beneath the sod

But some people do not think
That this is a blessing we should preserve
They damage this body with drugs
The blessing of God they pervert

Then when they have done their worst
They think others should fix the trash
Often parts are beyond repair
But they demand the sustaining cash

If we go into the water
Trying ourselves to drown
We must take responsibility
There can be nothing else found

For we are responsible
For what we say and do
This is an eternal truth
A truth that is true

WORLD IN TURMOIL

We live in a world in turmoil and sin
The beginning and end we cannot know
It is by the grace of God
That our soul can ever grow

As it is today
So it was when God's Son came
There are many, many differences
But the mind of man remains the same

We can but deal with the world as it is
This is where we live
But we will be eternally judged
By what we do, by what we give

So let us not be judged
By the doings of other men
For we are responsible for all
As our life did begin

THE WORLD OF MAN

We live in a world of men
We make a mess of things
We live by the will of God
Taking the good nature brings

We ask for more and more
Like the thirsty man water
But if we had all we wanted
We would have more than we ought to

There is only so much we need
To satisfy our desire
But selfish goals are not an end
If we got all we wanted
The results would be dire

So much of the our desires
Is not what we should have
But we will be judged
By what we are willing to give

GOD CHOOSE TO WORK WITH MEN

God choose to work with men
To teach us what we should do
He sent to us His only Son
To show us His Way is true

No other way is known to men
That is acceptable to the Most High
But to live as we should
So we might to God's throne draw nigh

HOW DO WE GET TO HEAVEN?

How do we get to Heaven?
When life's race we've run
Is there a magic, a holy way?
When the path had begun

There is but one way
Given by God above
It was, it is, it will be
An act of holy love

The death of the Holy Son
The raising on the third day
Was God's plan for salvation
Is God's Holy Way

THE BEGINNING OF ALL THINGS NEW

The beginning of all things new
Was coming of God's Son
When He gave us the Way
The holy Way to run

There was a time that God
In pity and in love
Chose to show us His Way
To be acceptable to Heaven above

We cannot know the cost
Paid by God's holy Son
When He was taken to the cross
Those who did thought they won

In the tomb He was laid
Passed to the other side and was dead
But it was the will of God
To follow what those of old said

On the third day
God raised Him to life anew
To show the world of men
Who He is, good and true

There are many times
When God touches the lives of men
Directs upon the path of life
Before we come to the end

We must ever be ready
To hear the will of God
That we may truly know His Way
Before we're beneath the sod

GOD SENT HIS SON

God sent His Son
To teach us His Way
The Way to heaven above
By the price His Son did pay

By the Way, by the plan
God had for His Holy Son
To live and teach and die
From before the world had begun

To die as God's Son did
Is not what I would choose
It was cruel death on the cross
To men the Son seemed to loose

Then God gave Him glory
Raised Him from the dead
So that by faith in Him
Men will not have death to dread

How should we feel about God?
We must love Him with all we have
How should we feel about the Son?
Gratitude for all He gave

So live our lives upon this earth
Do what God would have us do
By faith and the second birth
To God our life must be true

DO YOU REMEMBER?

Do you remember God's Holy Son?
Do you remember the Way He taught?
Do you remember the trials he suffered?
Do you remember your salvation He bought?

Jesus came, sent by our Holy God
Came to pay the price for our sin
That we might come to the feet of God
Might our heavenly life begin

If we would know the will of God
If we desire to holy be
Follow the teachings of Christ above
Part of the one in three

Remember as a baby He came
Remember the teachings from God above
Remember His life and death
Remember He showed God's love

Love the Lord God above
Love the Son He sent
Love the Holy Spirit here
Love the life to us He lent

WE MUST DO THE WORK

We must do the work of the Lord
The Lord of heaven and earth
The One who gave us His Holy Son
Sent by human birth

Some cannot believe that God
The Holy, all powerful One
In His holy plan for men
Would chose to send His Son

No man cam know the mind of God
Who in love sent His Son
That after this time
A new relationship had begun

Some believe that God would not allow
His Son to suffer and die
When told of this they puzzle
God, all powerful did allow, but why?

But God has a plan for all men
To be forgiven from every of sin
God raised the Son to life anew
The new relationship to begin

There are many things of nature
We cannot understand
But the actions of God above
Are beyond the comprehension of man

WHY SHOULD THE HOLY GOD

Why should the Holy God
Be concerned with the lives of men
Whose fortunes and lives
He knows from beginning to end

Why should the Holy God
Send His Holy Son
To live and teach and love
Till His mission on the cross was done

Why should the Holy God
Forgive the evil we do
When we turn from the right
Not worrying about what is good and true

Why should the Holy God
Let men seek His way
Teach us what to do
Help us know what to say

Why should the Holy God
Why indeed should He
Have a hope in men
Let us live, let us be free

LIMITED MEN AND WOMEN

Can we, as limited men and women
Find the will of the Almighty God
Can we, as humans, understand
What makes God - God

If we could understand
The God Who we hold dear
Wish to know His will
In faith, not in fear

How is it that we eternally look
For the holy path that we must trod
In order to go to heaven
Travel the path to the feet of God

It is by faith we search
From sun to setting sun
We know the way is there
Led by God's only, Holy Son

When this life has passed us by
When we may attempt eternity to know
We will find that we have walked our path
As into eternity we go

THE MERCY OF GOD

The mercy of God
Was sent to the lives of men
It healed the body and soul
Showed us how to begin

As it was thought out all time
So it is today
For those who do not follow
There is much they will eternally pay

God tells us how to live
Tells us what to say
Would that we should follow
Would that we did not have to pay

For God is a God of love
A God Who is holy and of peace
For it is the eternal Way
That we must follow and not cease

The future we can never know
The past is gone and done
But God has for us a Way
To make our life a holy one

So that we may live
Live and not eternally die
To go to the feet of our Holy God
His instructions we must ever try

So love the Lord with all your heart
Love also His Holy Son
For He has shown us the Way
As on life's road we run

IN THE WAR WITH EVIL

In the war with evil
The other side takes no prisoners
They fight to make us surrender
To fields of pleasure

But we must overcome
The temptation of the other side
And not be compromised
But on God's side abide

So take up the choice of right
Guard it with all your might
With mind, body and soul
Keep your inner self pure and right

Do not do what you know is wrong
Though it may appear right
For it is to God we answer
When ere we come into His sight

Hold to the best
Of Jesus Christ His Son
When we cross the great divide
We will the battle of right have won

WHERE IS THE LOVE OF GOD

Where is the love of God?
In this world of toil and sin
How can we find God's love?
Where do we begin?

God has shown His love
When He sent His only Son
To teach and guide us
As life's race we run

But to find God's love
To cash in on this state
We must follow the teachings of Jesus
With holy love, not hate

IN THE WAR FOR THE SOULS OF MEN

In the war for the souls of men
We must always seek the right
To be in the army of God
We must follow His eternal insight

There can be no slackers
Who go their own way
If they do not follow the will of God
For their error they shall pay

The Devil is cunning
The Devil is strong
Often his way seems the easy path
It is not right but wrong

So we must follow the will of God
In doing what is right
It will be by God's will
In the final judgment right makes might

STRUGGLE FOR RIGHT

Preparation for the struggle for right
Cannot be ignored
There are many things to do
Keep busy, don't get board

The commander is the Holy Son
Who has a plan so neat
When the struggle we undertake
Lack of preparation will lead to defeat

The Devil has many wiles
That can lead us astray
If we follow these as we would
We will have to pay

There is but one way we must go
It is the way that Christians know
That we must make the right
To go other ways will lead to eternal woe

Let us follow the way of God
Let us never falter
For the easy path
Will lead us to failure's altar

WHAT CAN WE GIVE GOD?

What can we give God?
Who sent His only Son
To be born of a woman
The act of holy love begun

He taught us how to live
He taught us how to love
As the Holy One from Heaven
The all powerful One above

In the world of toil and sin
God showed us His love
That by the Son's life
He gave His holy blood

A sacrifice for sin
An act of caring and love
To give us the way to live
In God's kingdom above

We are commanded to love God
Love also His Son
Only by the act of sacrifice
Could eternity be won

We cannot understand God's will
Except by faith and love
And find the eternal way
To Heaven above

MEN ARE A SELFISH LOT

Men are a selfish lot
From the beginning of life
We think that God above
Should settle our every strife

We pray "God help me always
In everything I would do"
Even when the outcome would be
Selfish, not to God true

But God has goals
For us, each and every one
Be faithful to His ends
As on the path of life we run

So we should not ask
"Is God on our side"
But rather we should seek
"Are we on God's side"

ONE WAY AND ONLY ONE

There is one way and only one
To be pleasing to our God
Given through the death of His Son
The holy way given the nod

How this can be
Is beyond the understanding of men
It is more than any can say
For in our understanding how to begin

For death seems so bad
As bad as anyone can pay
But it was the will of God
For us to follow the eternal way

For in the family of man
Death is our final rod
That any person can ever know
This is the way of God

WHEN GOD, THE ETERNAL KING

When God, the eternal King
Shall come upon this earth
Then we shall all be judged
Our only hope is the holy birth

The death of the body
Killed by the will of men
Is not what we should fear
But killing of our soul through sin

When in the eternal court
We will be judged for our sin
Fear the final judgment
When eternity doth begin

Those who kill the just
Who killed the Sons of God
Shall receive their just reward
When their body is beneath the sod

For God shall judge all men
By the eternal holy rod
The way is everlasting, eternal
The eternal will of our God

There is no second chance
To be free from evil we know
We think that God would not judge
If we would have it so

The time to repent is now
Now is the time we have
If we would be forgiven
It is by repentance we have

DO YOU KNOW MY GOD?

Do you know my God?
Do you understand?
Why He loves all men?
Try this, if you can

There is the love of God
Sitting on high
We must know how to live
If to Him we would draw nigh

We can know the will of God
As given by prophets of old
To make us a holy prize
Not to be in sin's hold

There are things we cannot know
We cannot live beyond our life
But if we follow the will of God
We will be speared eternal strife

CRY, CRY, CRY

Cry, cry, cry for the Son of God
Who came upon this earth
So that by His life and by His death
We may have the holy birth

But the death of the Son
Was not the end of His life
For by God's holy power
He was lifted above earth's strife

There is much we cannot know
There is more we cannot understand
Of why God, in His eternal mercy
Should care about the children of man

No one of our kind
Can set this in our mind
That we can only accept and praise
The blessings of our Lord to our soul bind

CHRISTIANS COMMEMORATE EASTER DAY

Christians commemorate Easter Day
Lord God established for us
We can know many things of life
But some we must just trust

So we celebrate the will of God
Who came into the world of men
Though it was not pleasant for Jesus
It did a new age begin

Let this be for you
The truth of the Holy Lord
That by the by and in the truth
It is always God's Holy Word

THE LANGUAGE OF HEAVEN

The language of Heaven
Is spoken by the Most High
It is understood by all men
When to God's throne we draw nigh

The language of Heaven
Tells of God's power and love
It is what we must respond to
If we would go to Heaven above

The language of Heaven
We will all learn when we're there
It is what we will understand
When we're scooped up in the air

IN A TIME LONG AGO

In a time long ago
In a village far away
Was born the King of life
Came to guide those who go astray

Did they know the time?
Did they know His name?
For as we walk the way of life
From Him it is the same

Go to the mountain
The mountain of God
Where the spirit is made whole
For those above the sod

There is no end of evil
In this world of men
But by the love of God
There is a way we can begin

So we must love the Lord
Lord of heaven and earth
Who sent His Holy Son
To give us spiritual birth

LET US PRAISE THE LORD

Let us praise the Lord
Let us praise His Holy Name
For He has sent His only Son
The pathway to heaven
Is in all ways the same

Would that we could be holy
Would that we could be acceptable to God
For in our own way
There is but one way to trod

No end to the toils of life
No end to the sins of men
Would that we were holy
To find a way to begin

For it is the Holy Lord
Who has given to those who can
Was shown by the Holy One
By the Son of Man

Those who can follow God's Way
Are those who are truly blessed
For they are attuned to God's will
They will have His eternal rest

THE WILL OF GOD

Do you know the will of God
The details of His plan
How He set a Holy Way
That is the hope for man

We hope to go to Heaven
When our life is done
We can find the Way to God
As through life we run

It was so long ago
When God sent His only Son
It is the loving way
To show men how life should run

He came as a tiny babe
On that Christmas Day
He loved the Lord
His respect he did pay

He grew to be a man
Walked His Way in life
Taught all to know the truth
To deal with human strife

Then He was killed
Though He had done no wrong
This made the devils sing
The evil victor's song

But God in His power
Raised Him to life anew
By this and only this
We may walk the Way that's true

So we may be made acceptable to God
So we may find the Way
For by the Son's life and by His death
Our debt of sin He did pay

LET NOT YOUR DESIRE

Let not your desire
Keep you on this earth
But surrender your life
To God's holy second birth

Let all understand
That God has a place for us
In God's Heaven above
For it is in that we trust

Let the words of my mouth
Let the actions of my hands
Let all my very being
Let me be acceptable when I can

Be attuned to the love of God
Do not turn away
For it is by our temptations
That we may be led astray

But by attuning to the will of God
We may find the Holy Way
That when we cross the great divide
We shall listen to what God has to say

HOW DO WE COUNT OUR WEALTH

How do we count our wealth
Both on earth and in Heaven above
On earth we count wealth in things
In Heaven by God's eternal love

On earth we must work for wealth
This is how we measure it
In Heaven how can we measure our wealth
It is by God's love we get what we get

We think that we are attuned to God's Way
We walk in the way we think right
But God showed His love by sending His Son
So let us be just in God's sight

The Son came, born a man Child
Lived so long ago
Taught and healed and died
So that to Heaven we might go

So let us truly praise the Lord
The things of the world pass away
But the wealth we have in Heaven
Will forever stay

So praise the Lord
Praise His holy name
Praise the Son of Heaven
That we may have forever
The love God has given

WE WISH TO KNOW

Men and women wish to know
The heavenly things from above
For God came by His Son
To show His eternal love

There is but one Way
Given by God's only Son
That to Heaven we might go
When life's race is done

So we must hang onto God's love
We must do what we can
There is no other way
To be made right by the Son of Man

THE HOPE WE ALL HAVE

There is but one hope we have
To be made right with the Most High
That in this life and in the next
We may to God draw nigh

We hope the hope
We must work the work
Given to us by the resurrected Jesus
Our duty we dare not shirk

Our life may seem long and drear
Our work may seem not to matter
But success is not what God commands
Ignoring the Way will souls scatter

It is to live the life and work the work
That is the mission of the saved
Give to all people everywhere
The truth that God to us He gave

MISSION TO MANKIND

God sent His Son on a mission to mankind
To come and show God's love
When ere His mission was established
He returned to Heaven above

Before He left the earth
He told his followers what to say
To guide the steps of people
To walk on Heaven's way

We must carry God's mission
To tell all people of the world
To teach them about the holy commands
The mandate of Heaven's truth swirled

Many actions of the children of men
Lead to a selfish way
But the Way of the Holy God
Is one, nothing else to say

Would that God came down to earth
Would that He walked among men
We can but humbly bow
As into the world He did send

We are sent into the world
By God's Holy Son
To tell all the world's great peoples
That eternity has begun

So march with the army of God
Into this world of sin
That by His power and by His word
We can show how salvation can begin

There is no other way
Known to the children of men
We have our marching orders
We are the ones that God doth send

WHAT DO YOU BELIEVE

What do you believe
About the Son from above
Who lived and taught and died
To show us God's love

He came to call the wicked
To clean up their act
But they crucified Him
That is a fact

God in His power and mercy
Raised Christ on the third day
That all may be born to heaven
And not for their evil deeds pay

How is it we wander?
How is it we worry
About God's everlasting judgment
It will come in a hurry

The power of God's holy Church
Is by the Holy spirit above
Is sent down to us
From Heaven in love

We must remember the promise
That God set for His desire
It is His Holy Spirit
That gives the Church its power

Love the everlasting God
Love also His only Son
It is by God's love we serve
And know that the Three are One

TO WHAT DO WE OWE OUR ALLEGIANCE?

To what do we owe our allegiance?
To what do we owe our love?
It is to God who sent his Son
To show us the way to heaven above

It was from long ago
It is from our God in love
We receive the message
Of the caring hand of Heaven above

There is much we cannot know
About the will of our Holy God
But there is much we owe
To the one who gives Heaven's nod

No one can know God's love
No one can truly understand
For by His power and by His love
He sent the Holy Son of Man

WHAT IS EASTER TO YOU?

What is Easter to you?
What does it truly mean?
For some it is colored eggs
For some it is things unseen

We do not just celebrate Easter
But remember the cost God did pay
To save the children of men
And give us heaven's way

Know that His death gave us the way
The way to be right with our Holy God
The cost was something we can not pay
Must be paid before we are beneath the sod

So truly worship our God
Worship in the holy way
We owe all to Him
This is all we need to say

WHENEVER EVIL STRIKES

Whenever evil strikes
Whenever evil hits us here
Then we seek God's face
Not be driven to despair

We cannot know the way of God
He does not shield us from all wrong
But shows us the way to be saved
For in His will we will to be made one

Why do bad things happen to the just
Why in the world of toil and sin
Do the just suffer wrongs by evil men
How does understanding begin

Jesus, the Son of God
Suffered more than we can ever know
But by His suffering we are made whole
By His example we may life's way to go

It is not the good times that tests
It is the problems we have
That to our soul adds strength
Teaches us what we must give

WHENEVER WE THINK OF GOD

Whenever we think of God
How we can be made right with Him
What do we believe we should do
To make our life according to His Way

If He would not have it so
Our hope would be in vain
For God is the Almighty One
To cross Him would be insane

By God's everlasting grace
He sent His only Son
To teach us how to be made right
With trust in the holy One

God's Son was born of a woman
In life He lived as a man
Taught the will of God
For us to follow, this is the demand

But as He lived upon the earth
As through His teachings He ran
The forces of evil killed Him
We must remember, if we can

But God fooled the murderers
He raised Christ from the grave
This is the eternal way
The path to Heaven God gave

NO MATTER HOW BAD

No matter how bad the event
Often good can come about
It was the death of a good and perfect Man
Though the world seems to doubt

There was an evil empire
Who wished to rule the world
They ruled by crushing all else
Their being was evil unhealed

But from this evil empire
Grew the organization of government
That we have today
That we might forever seek justice

It was by the empire so well established
That the Word could spread
To the ends of the earth
Travelers could go without dread

So went the Word of God
To every people, every land
The message of hope
The words of the Son of Man

As it was in the beginning
So it is today
The truth from the hand of God
We must follow or we will have to pay

There is the hope of salvation
Being forgiven from our sin
When to the final judgment
The Eternal Defender shall mend

But the hope of eternal forgiveness
Must not negate the doing of right
For by the teachings of the One
It must attune us to Heaven's might

THE WAY TO HEAVEN

There is but one way to Heaven
Given by our Holy Lord
Who in His eternal love
Sent His Son to give the word

The way chosen was one of pain and death
But as our Lord so loved us
That we may be by heaven loved
It is in this Holy Lord we trust

As God so loved the children of men
So we are to love Him above
This is the basis of our salvation
This is the One we love

THE WORLD OF MEN WAS WAITING

The world of men was waiting
For the first Easter day
They did not know the date
They did not know the price God would pay

But the rejoicing
Was from that day
It is the holy price paid
That God's Holy Son had to pay

We are sheltered from eternal death
By the will of the Most High
It is by the will of God
We can to God drew nigh

BEFORE THE AGE OF MAN

In the beginning
Before the age of man
There was, there is the Holy God
Set how the universe ran

But on Easter day
We commemorate the death
Of that kind, just and holy Man
Who did no evil but gave men rest

There is nothing like this
In any of the world's other faiths
For this is the basis of salvation
For this is God's grace

There was a time that men did kill
The Son of the Most High
They hung Him on a tree
Tried to make God's truth a lie

They placed in a grave
There his body did lie
Men thought this was the end
To negate the will of God they did try

But God did not leave Him dead
He was raised to life anew
That all who believe might be saved
The faith in Him is true

Now by His death and by His life
In the world of care
Gives us hope forever
In heaven when we get there

IN THE BEGINNING

In the beginning
Before the age of men
There was God in heaven
Who to the world did send

The truth of God's holy will
To those who would believe
In spirit and in truth
The joy of Heaven they could conceive

As it was in ages past
So it is today
That we have a mission
From God on what to do and say

God sent His holy Son
To live and work and die
So that by His work
We have a holy try

MEN SENT BY GOD

Men sent by God
Show us His holy will
We need to listen to God
Let our mind, body and soul be still

Would that we knew the path
Of the life we must trod
It will be for us the Way
That leads to the feet of God

We cannot find the way
If we do not follow God's will
We must ignore many other ways
Find the right path, pray and hold still

So follow the path
Set by God's Son
That in the end of all
It will be heaven we've won

CAN PEOPLE FIND THE TRUTH

When people search for answers
The truth they hope to find
They search the natural world
They hope the answers will be kind

People can find the truth
Given by the Most High
The truth in the spirit
If to peace we would draw nigh

People can find the truth
People can use the natural world
There is much we cannot know
But when they find the truth
They must act, must go

The past we lived and know
The present we have here
But the future has its truth
We will find when we get there

God makes the future
Where we will live
As a blessing for us
Life and hope He will give

BLESS OUR HOLY GOD

Bless our Holy God
Bless His only Son
Who came to show us the Way
As on life's path we run

The blessings of our Holy God
Are more than we can hope
So as we go through life
It will be on the upper slope

The way to be holy
Is by the will of God
That when into the future we go
We will follow the Holy Rod

IF GOD WERE A MAN

If God were a man
What kind of world would we have?
Would it be eternally just?
Would we be in a condition to give?

The answer to these questions
Is more than we can ever know
For the control of everything
Is something that makes the world go

If man controlled all
The world would be lost
For men are selfish
Men would make a poor eternal boss

But God controls the world
Rules this by His love
His mercy is all we can ask
From His person above

HEAVEN'S REVOLUTION

Heaven's revolution is a change life
A revelation in thought and mind
It guides our every action
It gives the hope that will shine

The revolution came with the Holy Son
Who taught the love of the Most High
That we may with the love of God
To His Holy Self draw nigh

Since this revelation came
The world has never been the same
It was a revolution in the thought of men
That made the world change

Revolution in our human relations
But the most profound revelation of all
Was the revolution of God's Son
Who came to save us from the fall

But the basic revolution was His church
That in this world of men
It was the revolution of God
We may find how to begin

The new and better way
Will be the new and perfect life
We must follow in the Way
That will keep us from eternal strife

THERE ARE MANY WAYS

There are many ways
That anyone may go
But the will of God
Is what we should seek to know

The beginning of mankind
Was the path of life
Sent by the will of Holy God
To calm human strife

The prophets through the ages
Told the Way of God
But men did not keep the Way
As they walked through sin's mud

Then, in accordance with His plan
He sent His Holy Son
To teach us the Way to live
As on life's race we run

There is no other way
We may be made right with heaven
For God came, will forever be
By the Son was given

For the Son lived with men
In holiness and in might
If we find His holy Way
It is our soul's delight

REJOICE

Rejoice
Again, I say rejoice
The Son of God has come
Has come to save our soul
Has come to comfort us
Has come to make us whole

Rejoice
Rejoice that the Holy One
Was sent from above
Was sent to show us the Way
Was sent to show God's love

Rejoice
Rejoice in all the world
To take the message to every man
To take the message to every woman
It is the will of God
So do good when ere we can

Rejoice
Rejoice, again I say rejoice
For God so loved you
For God so loved all mankind
That as we go through life
We shall the will of God find

Rejoice
Rejoice for the love of God
Rejoice in every way
Through life we must go
Because Christ did for our sins pay

Rejoice, rejoice, rejoice
There is no other way
But to follow our Lord
Great dividends it will pay

THE FORCES OF EVIL

The forces of evil
Fight the fight for our soul
They attack when we're weak
They leave us not whole

By the life of our Savior
Sent from God above
We can face the evil one
Make heaven's hope in love

So let us have faith
In the promises of Heaven
Accept the holy gift
Reject evil's enticing leaven

There is no beginning
Neither is there an end
For by God's Holy Rod
We receive the gift that God doth send

THE SUN COMES UP

The sun comes up in the morning
The sun sets every night
The Son of God came but once
To show us Heaven's light

There are those who claim the Lord
Who take His teachings on their lips
But use His Holy Name for selfish ends
This is sin that does God's kingdom hits

We are all accountable
For how we use God's word
For if we subvert the holy purpose
It is the worst thing ever heard

If we believe in the Son of God
Accepts His holy way
Then by our actions and by our words
Let Him guide us in all we do and say

PRAISE THE LORD

Praise the Lord
Praise His Holy Name
For He sent His only Son
Since He came nothing has been the same

Praise our Lord Who came
Came to make our spirit whole
Came by power so divine
Came to save our personal soul

Praise the Lord Who came
Came by His holy hand
Praise Him in all the world
Came as the Son of Man

Praise the Lord
Praise Him in all we say
Let us fully understand
There is no other way

Praise the Lord
Praise Him in all ways
Praise Him for His Son
Praise Him all our days

Praise the Lord
Praise Him for His great love
So loved He the world of men
That He sent His Son from above

Praise the Lord
Praise Him in every way
We must praise His holy name
Remember Him in every day

Praise the Lord
For He has come on earth
We praise Him for His Holy self
He gave us the way for the second birth

Praise the Lord
He has given us the Way
We can love Him, love Him, love Him
For He has shown us what we are to say

Praise the Lord
There is no other way
To show our love for Him
Throughout every moment of every day

THE TIME HAS COME

The time has come
To commemoration the power of God
The time that with His strong hand
Had freed the nation from Egypt's rod

The time came to eat the Passover meal
To draw the holy wine
To praise the Holy God
For the freedom they did pine

The bitter times of slavery
Were ended in one night
When God's death angel
Passed over the houses to set things right

When our Lord Jesus
Ate with His chosen men
He connected the old and the new
This is when the new world did begin

When the night was over
The events of Easter began
Christ was taken to be judged
Though He had no sin

Then why did they try Him?
By the secular and by the holy
We can judge the judges
But all was with God's plan there only

So Jesus died a death of shame
For the sins of men
So that we may be forgiven
Be free from eternal sin

There is no other way
By which our sins must be forgiven
This was set by God
So that we may be acceptable to heaven

So do not judge the people
The people of that day
For the events of Easter
Was chosen by God's way

INTO THIS WORLD

Into this world of toil and sin
God sent His only Son
So that by His life and by His death
Our salvation may be won

There were many deeds of love
God has done for men
Sending His only Son
Was where He chose to begin

The will of God for men
Was told by prophets of old
It was by the Holy Man
That we can Heaven take hold

We must believe in God
Believe in His holy Son
That on the pathway of life
We may know how we should run

The way of life may be long and dark
We cannot see the end
But by faith in our Holy God
We can learn how to begin

The light from our holy God
Is more than we can know
To show the way to live
The way our life must go

THE WORKING OF GOD

Mankind can do the work of God
Who demands from us our best
To do right, never wrong
To each other be blessed

No man may know all things
That God and nature demand
But we must try and work
Do the best we can

God works in various ways
To guide the acts of man
It is the holy way
That shows His demand

ALL PEOPLE HAVE SINNED

All people have sinned
We carry this guilt with us to heaven
For the Christian, when we get there
By a just and holy God can paradise be given

But how can we be made right with God
Is there a way our gilt can cease
God has given us a Defender, a Way
It is God's Son who pleads our case

God is a just and holy God
Who judges us for what we are
He will let the just into heaven
The unjust He will bar

We all know our sins
It is the burden of man
With Christ we can be forgiven
As we pass before God's Holy hand

GOD'S TIME

God's time is long and short
By the reckoning of mankind
For He has all eternity
To set His holy sign

God's time is a long time
For the universe from beginning to end
God's time is the short time
The subatomic events does nature rend

All times are God's time
The events that happen here in
God knows what happens
Can control, can change, can end

Man's time is a short time
It goes from day to day
We only have so many days
To follow in God's way

God chose to send His Son
To help us understand
How we should live
To behave right if we can

Because God cares for us,
Each and every one
Our total love to Him we must give
Unto God the Father of all
Unto the Son Who on earth did live

There are many the ways of men
Ways of women too
But what is, is - what was, was
There is nothing that is new

So we must work the work of right
As shown by the Holy One
For when we've passed over
Our work on earth is done

PRAISE THE LORD

Praise the Lord in heaven
Praise the Lord on earth
In His love and mercy
For He sent His Son by human birth

When the Son became a man
He was tempted in every way
He lived a perfect life
Overcame temptations every day

If I were the Son of God
Knew the power it would bring
I'd abuse the power for selfish ends
This would make Devils sing

But I am not the holy son
Not one with God's own power
I would not go my way
Cannot get all I desire

God chose the Way we must live
A Way taught by prophets and the Son
A way to live and work
So that in the end we will Heaven won

Let the words of my mouth
Let the actions of my feet
Be known as the follower of God
So that in the end it'll be God I meet

THE SPRING OF THE YEAR

The spring of the year
When all things are growing and new
Is a blessed time of year
It is when to God we must be true

The summer of the year
When days are long and hot
We do more than we would
To rest it is the thing we can not

The autumn of the year
When we reap what we did sow
We look back on what we did
We would be differently we now know

The winter of the year
We find a way to rest
The good that we would do
Is what would be the best

So it is with our life
The seasons of living in what we do
For unto the will of God
May our life be ever true

THERE ARE THINGS I WOULD DO

There are things I would do
There are places I would go
Some are good and holy things
There are things I would know

The past is in the purview of God
The present is where I live
The future is my hope, I pray
The things I have to God I'd give

So we continue
To live, to obey, to love
In the army of God
That we must follow the One above

ACCEPTED BY GOD'S SON

When we are accepted by God's Son
We are the elect of God
We must live a good and holy life
Do God's will that we would

How are we accepted by God's Son
To become God's elect
It is by faith and God's mercy
That we may have this effect

So becoming God's elect
Is by grace and mercy on God's part
It is by our belief and actions
That we can find God's heart

For God is a God of mercy and love
That none should experience the fall
It is following that works
As we answer God's eternal call

WHAT IS A CHRISTIAN?

What is a Christian?
What do we believe?
Do we really know?
How can this we achieve?

How can you tell a Christian?
In this world of sin
What actions do they take?
How do they begin?

A Christian begins with Jesus
The Son of God most high
Who taught the way of life
How to God we may draw nigh

Then He was killed
Nailed to a cross
His faithful followers
Thought all was lost

But He was raised to life anew
By His Father in heaven above
So that we may forever live
In the shine of God's love

Now many years have past
Since that fateful day
That our sins may be forgiven
His death for us He did pay

Let the will of God reign
Let the love of God bless
Save us from all evil
Save us from eternal distress

IN ALL THE WORLD

In all the world
We must answer God's call
There is only one God
Who made and loves us all

It is mankind's duty
To worship the Holy One on high
Who made the rules, that is the One
We can only follow and eternally try

For this Holy One on high
Who cares and loves us all
To whom we owe our very selves
Who saves us from the eternal fall

How do we know what we should do
That by the by and in the end
Will judge all by the eternity rules
Which is and was when all did begin

So love the Lord above
For He so loved us each and every one
If He did not love us and keep us
Our life would not have begun

Love the Holy Father of all
Love also the His Son
It is by the spirit of the living God
That our life, our world had begun

It is the suffering of the Son
Who came to the earth from above
To teach, to love, to die
To show us that indeed "our God is love".

SOME PEOPLE WANT GOD

Some people want God
To answer their every call
They say they will not believe
If He does not give them His all

But God is God
Creator of all mankind
It is He who has made us
No matter how we pine

So we can only worship God
Like a great and powerful king
Who knows all things
To Him our sublimations we bring

NO MAN CAN EVER BE GOD

No man can ever be God
Set above all we see
No matter what we'd rather
No other one can we be

For God is God
Above the works of man
No matter what we do
God controls more than we can

So follow the will of the Holy Father
Follow the teachings of His Son
That through life and in the end
It'll be Heaven we will have won

A LAND FAR AWAY

In a land far away
In a time long ago
God's perfect Son was born
Came so that God's will we might know

No man could understand
How God could send His Son
So that for those who believe
The Way to heaven could be won

We think we know all things
That man has lived and learned
But the more we find we know
The more questions we have earned

The more we know
The more questions we find
It seems a never ending cycle
But it is something we do not mind

Let not our heads be swollen
With knowledge of this life
For there are things we can never know
It is by what we worry we are blessed

In this life we have much to do
For those who would live
But it has many answers
When we choose to give

MADE RIGHT WITH GOD

In order to be made right with God
Our sins must be forgiven
While we live on earth
Before we enter heaven

In the First Covenant
God gave men a way to be made right
It was by the shedding of animal's blood
To be saved in God's holy sight

With the coming of the New Covenant
It is by the death of God's own Son
Who came and lived and taught
So that Heaven may be won

But both of the Covenants
The Old and the New
Is the sacrifice of something we treasure
Something both valuable and true

Let not the puzzle of God's holy plan
Confuse our understanding
For it is a holy way that stands
Through time now and the future remaining

HOW CAN THE HUMAN MIND

How can the human mind
Comprehend the infinite God?
How can the human heart
Receive the love of God?

How can the human mind
Understand the plan of God?
How can we as humans
Be made right with the Holy One?

There can be no comprehending
There can be no understanding
How we could be made right
There is very little we use
That will be made right in God's sight

But mercy is the will of God
Who sits upon the high judgment seat
For His mercy is our desire
It is a sentence that is hard to beat

So pray to the Lord above
Pray both day and night
For it is by His mercy
Our eternal life can be made right

GOD'S MERCY

There once was a man on trial
His lawyer kept saying
"We want justice, we want justice"
Finally the man said to his lawyer
"Sit down. If they gave me justice
They would hang me,
I want mercy, not justice."

So it will be with God
As we stand before the judgment seat
We want mercy not justice
For if we paid the price for all we did
It would be a bad fate we would meet

God's justice is eternal
From that end there is no appeal
For there is not a higher court
That could make the sentence not real

We must always understand
If before God we were given justice
It would not be good for it is forever
It is mercy we want God's trusty

God is a God of mercy
Giving us what we need
Does not give us what we want
No matter how we plead

If we were given all we wished
We would sit down in a crack
When we would try to get up
Our bottom would get a whack

So be thankful to our Lord
For all He to us doth give
Never complain to the Holy One
For He helps us to properly live

PRAISE BE TO GOD

Praise be to God
Praise His Holy Name
For He has saved our eternal soul
He is from age to age the same

Praise be to God's only Son
Who came and taught and died
Not for evil he had done
But for our sins He was tried

Praise be to the Holy Spirit
God's power on the earth
It gives the Church its power
Gives us the spiritual birth

Praise be the Holy Three
They are three yet one
For in the end of time
Their power will have just begun

We cannot understand this holy puzzle
How can God be three, yet one
It is not for us to understand
But this is how worship has begun

THE MIND OF GOD

If I could know the mind of God
Know His Holy Way
I should always know the right
Know always what to do and say

God's mind is above all men
Not just you and I
We can but worship Him
To His loving throne draw nigh

EASTER IS A COMBINATION

Easter is a combination
A celebration of love and hate
Love from the One above
Hate from men for the right
This can be forgiven by God's love

There is no justification
For those who abuse their power
But some thought no problem
To do whatever they desire

Easter is to remember Jesus
Who came and taught and was killed
By those who knew no better
To their souls this is billed

But God fooled them all
He raised Jesus from the dead
He showed His eternal power
So to follow Him is no dread

THE BRIGHT MORNING

The bright morning
Of the new day
The sun rose
As God's Son for our sins did pay

Sometimes it seems to me
This was a terrible waste
That for someone so good and holy
Should die in my place

But this was the plan of God most high
That for our sins Jesus did pay
For us to get hooked into this forgiveness
We must follow in His Way

God, the Father of all mankind
Of those who follow in His Way
Gives the most kind and glorious command
Taught us what we must do and say

There is no other one
Who could died for the sins of men
To make us right with God
Showed us how to begin

His suffering and His love
Is more than I can understand
For the forgiveness He gave to me
That God can forgive all the sins of man

But to receive this holy prize
We must truly from evil repent
This was the plan of God
When to us His Son He sent

WHEN WE THINK OF OUR HOLY GOD

When we think of our Holy God
We often think in human terms
We think God wants what we want
We think our desires are what He yearns

But God is God
Different from humankind
It is but our hope
It is for Him we pine

We should worship our Holy God
We try to have what we want
But we must always know the Holy will
Often what we want is something we don't

For there are many things we want
In this world we are in
That if we were to ever get
Would lead to eternal sin

But by the grace of the eternal God
We can be made right in the end
By following the teachings
We can a new life begin

SERVE THE LORD WITH GLADNESS

Serve the Lord with gladness
Serve Him every day
As we walk the road of life
Serve Him in every way

Follow His commands for life
Follow as we live and work
If we miss the way
Our holy duty we shirk

Many are our opportunities
To do God's holy will
It seems that we need but look
Else the opportunities we spill

So we should serve our Holy God
As we walk in life's way
For the end is our goal
When we cross over on that final day

There is but one Heaven
Where rules the will of the Most High
When our life's end comes
God's judgment will draw nigh

So live as we truly must
So live by the will of God
For we must find the way
To be right before we're beneath the sod

THE FUTURE IS BRIGHT

The future is bright
When we follow our Lord
He has given His commands
He has given His word

There is but one way in life
To be right with our Holy God
To find the way, the Holy Way
To love His holy rod

The Way was given by the Son of Man
Was given many years ago
It is by the will of God
That makes our Salvation so

Let us know the path of life
That we must ever trod
For in the end of this life
It leads to the feet of God

LIFE'S PATH

When life's path is trodden
And the end appears to come
We shall know the future is here
Wonder where life's time has gone

For the future is always there
Traveling from end to end
It is where we shall live
Sending us where life will send

So we must live our life now
Now is all we have
Time is nature's will
This is what eternity doth give

HELP

Help - I've been kidnapped by life
It seems that as time goes by
I live, have no other choice
No matter how I try

Would that I could control
What the future will bring
But as the future gets here
I get what I get, that's the thing

About the time I come to the end
When all seems to fit in place
It is time to begin again
On a new and different race

For if I would the end see
View over life's horizon
I would know more than I do
But the future is never given

So we must live as we ought
Live as given by the Most High
So that in the end
It'll be to the Heavenly thrown draw nigh

THE BEGINNING OF THE WILL OF GOD

The beginning of the will of God
Was when creation began
It was at the beginning of time
Before the age of man

The love of God for created men
Is beyond all we can know
No man has the understanding
About what makes the universe go

But there is much, much more
That fits the will of the Most High
More than we can ever know
As to the Holy One we would draw nigh

As we travel through life
In this world of toil and sin
God has given to us instructions
Of joy and of how to begin

Would that we should know
What is always right
So that all mankind
Can be acceptable in God's sight

So let us follow the will of God
In this earthly life
So when we cross the great divide
Our soul will enter God's sight

THE WILL OF GOD

The will of God was sent to earth
Through Jesus, the Christ, His Son
To guide us in our life
To show us how our life should be run

In the Old Covenant
God demanded animal sacrifice
He did not wish to kill the animals
But that all men should live right

The Old Covenant was made between
God and Israel as a whole
To worship and obey the One above
So that God could show His Holy will
And His eternal love

The New Covenant is made with each person
To follow God's Holy will
And have us follow His Way
To let our trembling soul be still

So let us worship in spirit and in truth
The One who loves us each and every one
That to help us follow His will
He sent His Holy Son

Let us know the way to go
As through our life we live
Attempt to follow God's Way
His holy will He did give

THERE IS BUT ONE WAY TO HEAVEN

There is but one Way to Heaven
Taught by Jesus Christ, God's Son
There are many ways that we may go
As on life's path we run

But following the wrong way
Is not an option that we should go
To be made right with God
It is God's will we must know

For in the end of life
When judged at God's throne
We will find that our evil deeds
To all will be made known

In Christ we have the Great Solicitor
Who will before God defend us
For if we received justice
Our fate would be a bust

But it is by the grace of God
As given through His Son
That forgiveness is given
As into eternity we run

ALL PEOPLE MUST WORK

All people must work
To do the will of God
That when their end comes
They'll be at peace beneath the sod

For though the body decays
Can never return from the grave
If their spirit is not right
Their eternity shall be grave

When life has past
And we've crossed the great divide
There is no undoing the evil we've done
There is no place to hide

So we should live our life
As though we're standing before God's throne
For at that time and in that place
All we've done shall be known

FOLLOW HIS TEACHINGS

Know that we must follow the teachings
Of the One sent from above
When we follow in God's Way
We shall find God's eternal love

Would that our God
Was by all men known
But the evil that we do
Can block us from Heaven's home

So repent from your evil ways
If ever you turn from the right
God will, God shall judge us all
By His justice and might

ABOUT THE AUTHOR

Richard Gold has been a Christian for many years and has been writing Christian poems since 2008. He was inspired to write these poems by the past Christmas and the Easter season in which the poems commemorate the joy of the resurrection and the salvation that this brings.

Gold was born in Bartow Florida and has attended college and worked for the Government for 40 years. He is now retired which has given him the time necessary to produce poems among other things.